READING
THEN & NOW
IN COLOUR

STUART HYLTON

MODERN PHOTOGRAPHY
BY MICHAEL HYLTON

The
History
Press

First published in 2011

The History Press
The Mill, Brimscombe Port
Stroud, Gloucestershire, GL5 2QG
www.thehistorypress.co.uk

British Library Cataloguing in Publication Data.
A catalogue record for this book is available from the British Library.

ISBN 978 0 7524 6325 4

Typesetting and origination by The History Press.
Printed in India
Manufacturing managed by Jellyfish Print Solutions Ltd

CONTENTS

ACKNOWLEDGEMENTS

My particular thanks go to David Cliffe and his colleagues at the Local History Library at Reading Central Library for their support for the first edition of this book. Reading Museum Service allowed me to reproduce a number of the images from the collection of historic *Reading Chronicle* photographs which they hold. The *Reading Chronicle* itself allowed me to use a number of their more modern archive photographs. I was also helped by a number of private collectors in preparing the first edition and in particular I would like once again to record my thanks to Richard Reed, Graham Parlour and John Griffin. I would also like to thank the authorities at St Peter's church, Caversham, for allowing me access to the church roof in order that I might take a photograph from it.

Last, but by no means least, I would like to thank my son Michael, who took the colour photographs of modern Reading.

ABOUT THE AUTHOR

Stuart Hylton was born and grew up in Windsor, Berkshire. He worked as a town planner in Reading between 1980 and 1998 and since then has been head of strategic planning and transport for all of the Berkshire local authorities. Stuart is married with two grown-up sons, one of whom took the colour photographs for this book. His writing interests have led to numerous appearances on radio and television and he used to write a regular local history column for his local newspaper.

INTRODUCTION

Over a period of about twenty years I have written about various aspects of the history of Reading, illustrating the books with some of the rich variety of photographs and drawings of the town that exist in public and private collections. Many other books have also added to the ever more fully documented history of this ancient town.

This book, the first edition of which came out in 2000, is a comparison of the Reading of the past with the town of today. Anyone who has lived in Reading for any length of time will be conscious of the dramatic changes it has undergone and continues to undergo. Many parts of the town are virtually unrecognisable as the place I got to know when I came here in 1980.

In the past, the modernising tendency showed little respect for the town's history. There was a stage during the 1960s when, it was said, Reading's listed buildings were being demolished at the rate of one a week. Equally sadly, the modern buildings that took their place proved in all too many cases not to be worthy successors. Their looks soon dated badly, their fabric began to crumble and they proved unable to adapt to the changing demands of their occupiers. Buildings I saw going up – as a child visiting Reading or even, in some cases, as an adult living in the town – are already being torn down and replaced, such is the economic buoyancy of the area. All the signs are there that this pace of change will continue unabated.

The happier side of this is that a lot of the more recent development has started to show a greater degree of respect for its historic neighbours. Also, extensive efforts are now being made to preserve the town's architectural heritage and find new uses for it where necessary. The proposals to demolish the old town hall led, in 1962, to the formation of the Reading Civic Society and to a more active conservation lobby in the town. Among its other achievements, it was instrumental in promoting the restoration of the town hall as an arts, leisure and conference centre, and the re-use of the old Mansion House in Prospect Park. Other buildings have also found new uses – the old shire hall is now a court, the old coroners' court is part of an office development and the former railway station is now a pub.

Another thing that you see as you compare the old images with the new is how affluent the town has become. Poverty can clearly be seen in the physical fabric of Reading in bygone years; buildings which we would today regard as derelict, and in all probability unsafe, were still in active use, even in the very heart of the town centre. The picture of Cross Street in 1887, shown on pages 10–11, shows the street that formed the most direct vehicular link between the railway station and the retail heart of the town in Broad Street, prior to the opening of Queen Victoria Street in 1903. This was the front door of the town. Can you imagine this as the gateway to Reading town centre today?

THE VIEW FROM
THE TOWER

OVER 250 YEARS separate these three images of Reading, as seen from the top of St Peter's church, Caversham. The first (above) was drawn in about 1750 when George II was still King, America was still a British colony and the Industrial Revolution was yet to begin. A wide expanse of fields separated Reading and Caversham, and the church towers of St Laurence's and St Mary's dominated the skyline. The second image (opposite above) is a photograph taken about a century later – the young Queen Victoria was now on the throne. The two settlements are still far apart but the church towers now share the skyline with the early factory chimneys of Huntley & Palmer, along with other buildings. We can date this photograph to before 1869 by the presence of the old 'half and half' Caversham Bridge. The photograph would have been taken from the old wooden church tower, built after the original was damaged during the Civil War battle in this area. The large house in the foreground was Caversham Court, home of the Simonds, a brewing family.

IN THE MODERN photograph below, the two settlements are much more closely linked and tall office buildings have become the dominant feature of the town. Caversham Court was demolished in the 1930s but its gardens remain as a public amenity.

THE RAILWAY STATION

ORIGINALLY BOTH THE up and down platforms of the station were on the south side of the track (which was built on an embankment, well above the surrounding floodplain). The old photograph shows the down platform in about 1850. A second line, the South-Eastern Railway, reached Reading in 1849, linking it to Waterloo via a second terminus, which only closed in 1965.

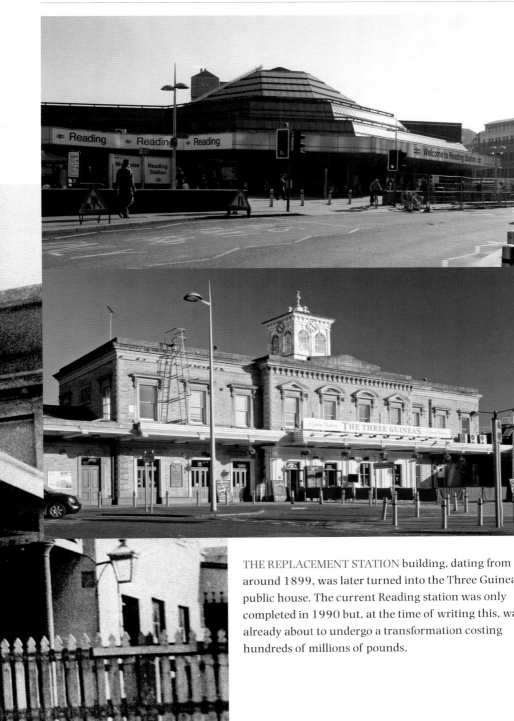

THE REPLACEMENT STATION building, dating from around 1899, was later turned into the Three Guineas public house. The current Reading station was only completed in 1990 but, at the time of writing this, was already about to undergo a transformation costing hundreds of millions of pounds.

CROSS STREET

A DERELICT-LOOKING CROSS Street (previously known as Gutter Lane) photographed in 1887 (below). At that time (and until 1903 when Queen Victoria Street opened) it formed the major route between the station and the town's main shopping district on Broad Street.

CROSS STREET HAD its origins in some of the 'town planning' of medieval Reading, linking the newly formed High Street (what we call Broad Street today) to New Street (now Friar Street). Nowadays it is considerably more spruced up than in Victorian times but has become something of a backwater among Reading's shopping attractions.

CAVERSHAM BRIDGE

A BRIDGE IS known to have existed at the site of the present Caversham Bridge from as early as 1231. For many centuries, as the old photograph opposite above shows, it took the form of this distinctive 'half and half' bridge, reflecting the fact that two separate authorities, in Caversham and Reading, were responsible for its construction and upkeep. For a time during the Civil War the Reading side was a drawbridge. In 1869, it was replaced by the narrow, all-iron structure shown in the old photograph opposite below.

THE IRON BRIDGE was unable to cope with the growing traffic, and as part of the 1911 agreement to merge Reading and Caversham the new authority was committed to build the current bridge seen in the modern photograph above. However, the distractions of the First World War meant that it was not opened until 1926.

SOUTHAMPTON STREET

THE VIEW OPPOSITE above is of a Southampton Street (then known as Horn Street) as it was in 1823. St Giles' church, which dates back to 1191, still has the replacement spire it was given following the damage it suffered from artillery during the siege of Reading in the Civil War.

BY THE TIME of the second illustration of 1887 (opposite below), Southampton Street had acquired its modern name and St Giles' church had undergone its refurbishment and got its current steeple. When it was first built, St Giles' church was cut off from the town centre by a host of streams and marshes associated with the River Kennet.

NOWADAYS, AS CAN be seen in the 2011 photograph above, Southampton Street is cut off from the town centre by the maelstrom that is the Inner Distribution Road. The trees and shrubs that have been planted on the right-hand side of the road brighten up an otherwise unremarkable scene today.

KING STREET

THE OLD PHOTOGRAPH below looks eastwards along King Street in 1866. King Street was built in 1760. Until then it had had a row of dilapidated houses running down the middle, dividing it into Sun Lane and Back Lane. Kings Road was built some time before 1832, marking a new direction of growth for the town, but at this time King Street did not lead directly into it but joined it via Duke Street. The picture is taken from the eastern end of Broad Street, which

in the early nineteenth century was also divided into two narrow streets. Their names – Fishe Strete and Bucher's Row – give some clue to the trades conducted there.

BY THE TIME of the modern picture, Barclays Bank occupied the large white building just visible in the centre of the picture. But it was originally built by the local Simonds brewing family in 1836, as part of their diversification into banking. Their brass nameplate can still be seen on the building.

MARKET PLACE

MARKET PLACE WAS created by the Abbot of Reading as a piece of medieval town planning, designed to usurp the town's traditional market place in St Mary's Butts. It has hosted many important events in the town's history, including a pitched battle between supporters of

William of Orange and James II, during the misnamed 'Bloodless Revolution' of 1688. In this 1823 view, St Laurence's still has the Blagrave Piazza along its south side. Built in 1619 and not demolished until 1868, it housed the town's instruments of justice (stocks, pillory etc.) and was apparently the scene of much vice and depravity!

TODAY, SOME OF the buildings that were there during the battle of 1688 still survive, but the area is notable mostly for the acts of vandalism committed in the name of early post-war redevelopment.

DUKE STREET

DUKE STREET, FROM the High Bridge in 1823 (opposite above), 1910 (opposite below) and 2011 (above). The duke in question is Edward Seymour, Duke of Somerset, the uncle of King Edward VI and Lord Protector during Edward's minority reign (1547–53). Somerset was also Lord of Reading and was responsible for starting the destruction of Reading Abbey after the Reformation. Note the sentry box on the far side of the bridge which would have been occupied by a nightwatchman, forerunner of the local police force (which was not formed until 1836).

THE OLD PHOTOGRAPH opposite below shows the view from the opposite pavement in 1910, on what is clearly a busy day.

TODAY, ALL THAT survives of the pre-Victorian street scene is the line of the street and the High Bridge. Designed by Robert Brettingham, whose other projects included Longleat House, the bridge dates from 1787 and is one of the town's handful of Scheduled Ancient Monuments.

ABBEY GATEWAY

ALTHOUGH THE ABBEY Gateway is thought of as part of the medieval abbey, it owes much of its appearance today to the Victorians. The old photograph below shows it much as Jane Austen would have seen it when she attended school there in 1785. After centuries of neglect, the gateway collapsed during a storm in 1861.

ABBEY GATEWAY UNDERWENT what Nikolaus Pevsner describes as a 'drastic restoration' at the hands of eminent Victorian architect Sir George Gilbert Scott. The results can be seen in the modern photograph opposite.

ST LAURENCE'S CHURCH
FROM FORBURY GARDENS

THE PICTURE ABOVE shows St Laurence's church, as seen from what is now the Forbury Gardens. We can date the picture to after 1786 by the presence of the old town hall to the right of the image. The land in the foreground was originally part of the outer courtyard of the abbey, and part of it was used at this time as a muckheap by the town's street-sweepers. The area was acquired by the council and landscaped in 1855. In the old picture, the church tower dominates the skyline.

THIS PHOTOGRAPH (RIGHT) shows the gardens in their Edwardian elegance. The lion at their centre commemorates the bravery of 328 members of the Royal Berkshire Regiment at the Battle of Maiwand in the Afghan wars of 1879–80. Their rearguard action allowed their comrades to escape.

TODAY, LARGE COMMERCIAL office buildings and trees have tended to dwarf the view of the church.

NEWTOWN FROM
THE BRIDGE

THE SUBURB OF Newtown was built in the mid to late nineteenth century, mainly to house the workers at the nearby Huntley & Palmer biscuit factory. The old photograph on the left is the view of part of the area as seen from the King's Road Bridge over the River Kennet. It was taken in 1938, when new safety railings were about to be installed. The left-hand side gives an impression of the industrial dereliction that used to line much of the town's waterways.

THE AREA WAS redeveloped after the Second World War. This has been the result of a long-term policy on the part of the council, which they have pursued on all their waterways for over thirty years, to open them up to the public.

THE HOSPITIUM OF ST JOHN

THE HOSPITIUM OF St John was built in 1196 as part of the medieval abbey where visitors would be entertained. From about 1486 the ground floor was used as the schoolroom of Reading School and it has variously served over the years as a guildhall, stables, a Civil War gunpowder store and a home to the Reading University College, which would eventually become Reading University. The first picture shows it in about 1885, prior to its Victorian 'restoration' at the hands of architect Slingsby Stallwood.

BY THE TIME of the modern photograph above, it had undergone a further refurbishment as part of the adjoining office development. The churchyard, which it borders, also contains the remaining parts of the west window of the church, blown out in the bombing raid of 1943, and a monument to one Henry West, a carpenter killed in a freak whirlwind whilst getting Reading's railway station ready for its opening in 1840.

CEMETERY JUNCTION AND PUBLIC TRANSPORT

IN 1877, THE Imperial Tramways Co. set up a horse-drawn tram service between Cemetery Junction and Brock Barracks on the Oxford road. Within three years it was carrying 12,000 people per week. This tram is seen at Cemetery Junction in 1903, shortly before the service was taken over by the local authority and the horses replaced by electric vehicles. The wires for the new trams can be seen overhead.

THE CEMETERY, WHOSE gateway still forms a landmark in this part of town today, was opened by the private Reading Cemetery Company in 1843 in response to the gross overcrowding that existed in the town's churchyards. The council did not seek to acquire it until 1887. Its plots were strictly segregated according to the religion of the deceased.

BROAD STREET JUNCTION

FOR THOSE NOT on a tram route, horse buses – not far removed from the old stagecoaches – remained the main means of public transport. The old photograph below, taken at the junction of Broad Street, St Mary's Butts and West Street just before the start of the twentieth century, shows a horse bus turning up West Street. Pedestrians at that time took their chances crossing the street in competition with the other traffic.

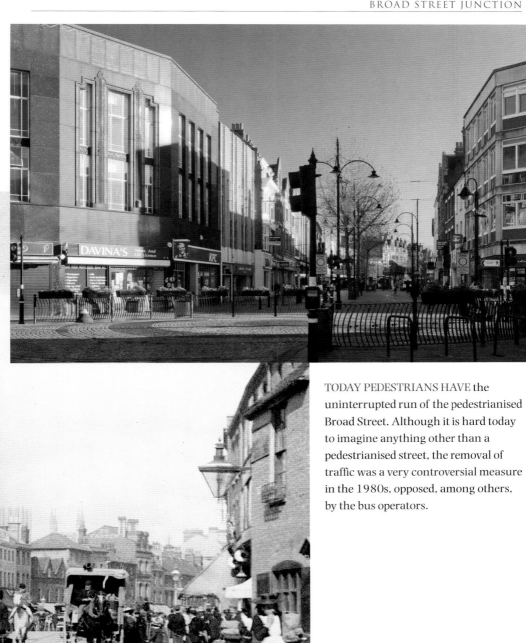

TODAY PEDESTRIANS HAVE the uninterrupted run of the pedestrianised Broad Street. Although it is hard today to imagine anything other than a pedestrianised street, the removal of traffic was a very controversial measure in the 1980s, opposed, among others, by the bus operators.

BROAD STREET

BROAD STREET HAS long been the retail centre of the town. In medieval times sheep would be penned along the street on market day. This is a view of Broad Street looking westwards in about 1960. At that time pedestrians and general traffic still competed for space in the street. Note the three-wheeled lorry, once a familiar sight on the roads and used for the local distribution of rail freight.

BROAD STREET WAS developed in the twelfth century as a bit of medieval town planning, actively promoted by the Abbot of Reading. Its purpose was to try and lure trade away from the town's existing market in St Mary's Butts to the new one in Market Place. It is hard to imagine today, but it would once have been filled with the sheep and cattle pens of the town's livestock market.

BROAD STREET: READING'S BUS DEPOT

A REMINDER OF the days after general traffic had been removed from Broad Street, but pedestrians still took their lives in their hands crossing it as it had become the town's main bus terminus. The photograph on the left was taken in 1967 while the town's trolley buses were in the process of being withdrawn and shows one of the one-man buses that would replace them. They were initially unpopular, dismissed as 'cattle trucks'.

ITS MODERN EQUIVALENT is seen above, unloading passengers in St Mary's Butts, about the nearest point to Broad Street that they can now reach since pedestrianisation. But the closure of Broad Street to traffic did not deal the fatal blow to public transport that some forecast.

HEELAS

THE STORE THAT younger shoppers refer to as John Lewis will forever be known to its older customers as Heelas. Daniel Heelas founded his draper's shop on Minster Street in 1854. They diversified and expanded, and by the time of this first photograph in about 1870 they had a presence on Reading's main Broad Street frontage. The Heelas store can be seen on the right. Heelas was sold by the family in 1947 and became part of the John Lewis Partnership in 1953.

HEELAS' LARGEST EXPANSION, however, came in the 1980s when this ambitious extension was completed on its original Minster Street frontage. The building tries not to be too much of a dominant backdrop to the neighbouring St Mary's church. Heelas was the last of the town's department stores to retain at least its local connection through its name. Bulls, McIlroys and Welsteeds all expired after the war and today only Jackson's survives as a genuinely local business.

UNION STREET –
'SMELLY ALLEY'

UNION STREET, UNDERSTOOD to have been named in commemoration of the Act of Union between England and Scotland in 1707, links Broad Street and Friar Street. It is better known as 'Smelly Alley' because of the variety of flavoursome trades traditionally carried out along it. The photograph on the left shows it as it was in about 1908.

IT IS LITTLE changed in outward appearance today but, thanks to the modern marvel of refrigeration, it is considerably less smelly than it used to be.

CASTLE STREET

CASTLE STREET WAS once a thriving shopping district as the old photograph below, dating from around 1910, shows.

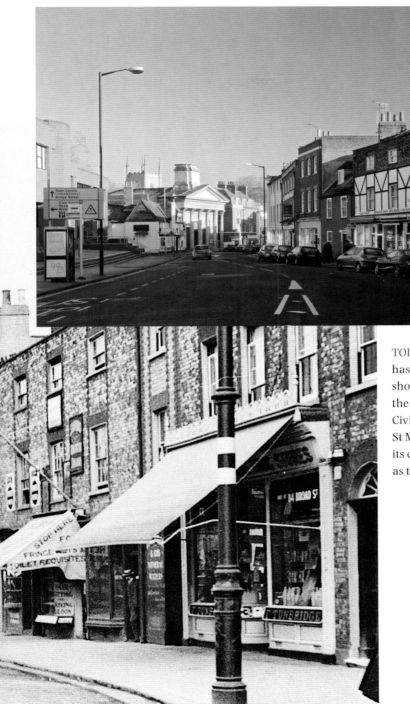

TODAY CASTLE STREET
has lost much of its
shopping, partly due to
the development of the
Civic Centre complex, and
St Mary's church has lost
its curious steeple, known
as the 'pepper box'.

LONDON STREET

LONDON STREET IS seen in the old photograph below looking northwards from the junction with South Street *c.* 1882. It was once an important part of the town's shopping district.

TODAY IT IS somewhat cut off from the centre by the Inner Distribution Road. London Street (and other streets in Reading) are among the first streets anywhere in the world to be photographed. This was because photographic pioneer William Henry Fox-Talbot set up his photographic establishment at what is now No. 55 Baker Street, Reading, in 1843–4. His practice of working in the dark and buying large quantities of paper led locals to conclude that he was a banknote forger!

THE SUN INN AND
ST MARY'S CHURCH

READING BECAME A stopping off point for eighteenth-century travellers between London and the spa at Bath, made fashionable by Queen Anne. Many coaching inns grew up to meet their needs. The Sun in Castle Street had its stables underneath the bedrooms – a curious arrangement

which may have helped with the heating of the rooms, but not with their ventilation.

ST MARY'S IN Castle Street was established in 1798 as a result of a dispute between the congregation of St Giles' church in Southampton Street and their extremely dull new vicar. It is built on the site of Reading's medieval common gaol. Prisoners had to pay the gaoler for the 'privilege' of being incarcerated and those without independent means were reduced to begging to passers-by through a grating set into the street above their subterranean cells.

PRINCE OF WALES INN, PROSPECT STREET

THE PRINCE OF Wales, at the top of Prospect Street in Caversham, was at one time the terminus for the horse bus services into Reading. The photograph on the right was taken in about 1900 when Caversham was still part of Oxfordshire, independent of Reading. The two were merged in 1911.

THE DIVISION OF Reading and Caversham into separate administrations caused many problems over the years, not least of them being disputes over the upkeep of Caversham Bridge. The desire to get

a modern replacement for the old iron bridge was one of the factors that led to the merger. Another was Caversham wanting to make use of more of Reading's facilities, such as its new fever hospital (Caversham suffered its own epidemic of scarlet fever in 1908).

THE THREE TUNS, WOKINGHAM ROAD

THE THREE TUNS on Wokingham Road has a long history. At the beginning of the nineteenth century, a ramshackle group of volunteer militia called the Woodley Cavalry used to meet there to plan how to repel Napoleon's army should he ever have the temerity to invade. They were led by the only prime minister Reading has so far produced, Henry Addington, later Viscount Sidmouth.

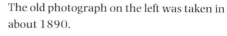

The old photograph on the left was taken in about 1890.

THE BUILDING HAS been replaced in the meantime but the name remains. Reading has not always been fortunate in the national figures it has produced. The aforementioned Henry Addington had a tough act to follow – Prime Minister William Pitt – and was generally judged to be among the least successful occupants of the post. Our only Archbishop of Canterbury, William Laud, ended up being executed by parliament during the Civil War.

THE MARQUIS OF GRANBY,
CEMETERY JUNCTION

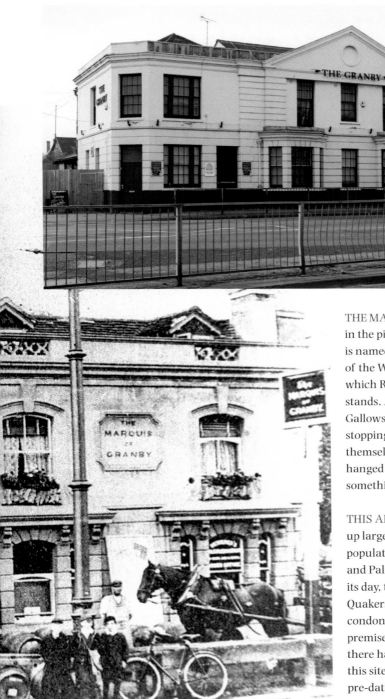

THE MARQUIS OF Granby (seen in the picture on the left *c.* 1906) is named after the one-time owner of the Whiteknights estate on which Reading University now stands. At one time it was called the Gallows Tavern and was the final stopping point for prisoners to fortify themselves while on their way to be hanged – last orders really meant something in those days.

THIS AREA OF Reading grew up largely to serve the working population of the nearby Huntley and Palmer biscuit factory – in its day, the world's largest. Being Quakers, the Palmers would not have condoned the building of licensed premises on land they owned. But there had been an inn on or near this site since at least 1790, long pre-dating the factory.

THE MERRY MAIDENS,
SHINFIELD ROAD

THE MERRY MAIDENS on Shinfield Road (seen in the picture on the left *c.* 1924) took its name from the series of stone female busts that once adorned its façade. The name may in turn have come from a Bronze Age stone circle in Cornwall. Legend has it the maidens concerned were caught dancing in a circle on the Sabbath (which was strictly taboo) and were punished by being turned into stone.

THE STONE BUSTS are gone today and the pub has apparently ceased to be merry, now being known simply as the Maidens. The buildings in the two pictures are little changed but the 1924 street scene has a much more rural air about it.

CAVERSHAM BRIDGE HOTEL

CAVERSHAM BRIDGE HOTEL was where the members of the Caversham Council celebrated their last night of independence in 1911 before they lost their battle and were incorporated into Reading. The tram service stopped here because Caversham Council would not meet the cost of extending it into their territory.

CAVERSHAM BRIDGE HOTEL was redeveloped in the 1980s and is now part of a multinational chain. The old photograph on the left was taken in about 1910, when it was apparently still safe for small boys to stand in the middle of the road.

ST MARY'S BUTTS/
BRIDGE STREET

IN MAY 1926, the nation was in the grip of a general strike. Reading was affected and there were demonstrations against the strike-breakers who volunteered to drive the trams under

police protection. In the photograph on the left, women demonstrators can be seen making their way along St Mary's Butts. The strikers made much propaganda out of female support for their cause.

TODAY, THE PEOPLE most likely to be shouting the odds are market traders in nearby Hosier Street. This, like a number of Reading's street names, denotes the trades originally carried on in them. Silver Street, for example, was not the home of silversmiths but of sieviers – the makers of sieves.

ST MARY'S CHURCH

ST MARY'S HAS a history dating back to the year AD 978 when a nunnery was built on the site of what now is the church. The earliest part of the church still standing today is a Norman doorway in the north wall. Most of it was rebuilt in about 1551, using materials from the demolition of Reading Abbey. It was further restored in the nineteenth century.

THE OLD PICTURE shows the church as seen from the south-west *c.* 1890, by which time both the church and its setting had just about reached their modern form. The earliest photographs of the church, taken in the 1840s, show windows set into the roof of the un-modernised building. By the time of the 1890 photograph, the slum buildings that separated the church from St Mary's Butts had been demolished.

GREAT KNOLLYS STREET

MEMBERS OF THE Berkshire Yeomanry assemble in Great Knollys Street in August 1914, prior to their embarkation for France and a war in which cavalry would play little part (below). The street takes its name from the Knollys family, who owned the land on which it was built (as well as large parts of the rest of Reading). Sir Francis Knollys (or Knolles as the name was then spelt) lived in the great house at Caversham Park and was married to a cousin of Queen Elizabeth I.

A CENTURY LATER, and the motor vehicle had well and truly supplanted the horse as a means of transport, in peace and war. Today the livestock market has gone from Great Knollys Street and the only horse power to be seen there is to be found in the buses going in and out of the Reading transport depot.

JUBILEE FOUNTAIN,
ST MARY'S BUTTS

PART OF THE Royal Berkshire Regiment pause in St Mary's Butts to water their horses in August 1914 (below). The monument commemorates Queen Victoria's Golden Jubilee in 1887 and can still be seen in St Mary's Butts.

TODAY, THOUGH, ITS function as a horse trough has long been superseded. Queen Victoria is also commemorated in the statue outside the old town hall. It is said that it faces towards the railway station because she disliked the town and could not wait to leave it!

ST MARY'S BUTTS

UNTIL ABOUT 1877 a row of slum buildings stood in the middle of St Mary's Butts at its southern end. A further row of buildings, including almshouses dating back to the fifteenth century, used to back onto the churchyard, until they were demolished for road widening in 1886. They can

both be seen in this view of St Mary's Butts, taken just before 1877. The Allied Arms public house, on the left of the picture in front of the church tower, is one survivor from that period and dates back to the sixteenth century, though its façade is a later addition.

ST MARY'S BUTTS is one of the oldest parts of the town. It is where the first street market used to take place. It is also where, on given holidays, the men of Reading were required by law to report for longbow practice to prepare them for possible military service. Reading men were among the archers at the battle of Agincourt.

CHEAPSIDE

THE READING HOME Guard parade along Cheapside during the Second World War (left). At that time Cheapside was one of the town's major entertainment venues. In the background you can see the Palace Theatre. This was built in 1907 and survived Hitler's bombs only to be destroyed by post-war competition from the television. A youthful Cliff Richard was one of the last acts to perform there, before it was demolished for office development in March 1962. Beyond it is the Odeon cinema, which met a similar fate around the turn of the century.

TODAY, VENUES SUCH as the Hexagon and the multiplex cinema in the Oracle provide some of Reading's prime entertainment, and Cheapside has become a relative backwater of the town's commercial centre.

ST LAURENCE'S CHURCH AND THE OLD TOWN HALL

BOMB DAMAGE TO the town hall and St Laurence's church after Reading's most serious air raid of the Second World War in February 1943. A single Dornier bomber swept over the town,

dropping a stick of bombs between Minster Street and the town hall, killing forty-one people. The bomber was thought to have been shot down with the loss of all its crew before it reached the coast.

TODAY, ALL THE buildings are restored to their original condition, although the town hall narrowly escaped more serious damage in the 1960s when plans to demolish it were successfully resisted by, among others, the newly-formed Reading Civic Society.

TOWN HALL SQUARE AND
MARKET PLACE

THE TOWN HALL Square in 1945 (left). Most of the wartime bomb damage has been cleared away but redevelopment has not yet started. This was the view from in front of St Laurence's church, looking towards Market Place during the VE Day celebrations. The bomb-damaged area on the right of the picture is where much of the loss of life took place during the 1943 air raid.

THE SITE, WHILST still derelict, was once promoted as the possible location for one of those new-fangled multi-storey car parks but was instead occupied by the rather unprepossessing office and shopping development seen in the modern photograph above.

CASTLE STREET

GOOD FRIDAY IN 1958 and Castle Street is the focal point of a demonstration (right). Campaigners for nuclear disarmament are seen making their way from London to the Atomic Weapons Research Establishment at Aldermaston in what became an unusual Easter pilgrimage during the 1950s and '60s.

READING APPARENTLY ONCE had a castle, though it is thought to have been destroyed as early as 1152 by Henry, Duke of Normandy. Nobody today knows even where it stood – although somewhere in the vicinity of Castle Street or Castle Hill seems a reasonable bet.

ST PETER'S CHURCH, CAVERSHAM

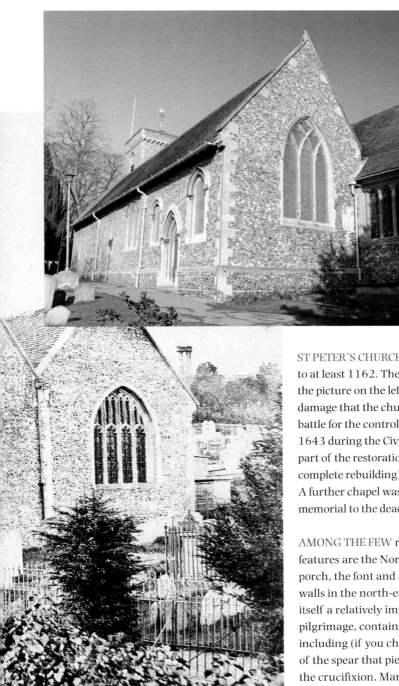

ST PETER'S CHURCH, Caversham, dates back to at least 1162. The wooden tower shown in the picture on the left was built following the damage that the church suffered during the battle for the control of Caversham Bridge in 1643 during the Civil War. It was replaced as part of the restoration (for which read virtually complete rebuilding) of the church in 1878–9. A further chapel was built in 1924 as a memorial to the dead of the First World War.

AMONG THE FEW remaining medieval features are the Norman inner doorway of the porch, the font and a couple of twelfth-century walls in the north-east corner. St Peter's was itself a relatively important place of medieval pilgrimage, containing many religious relics including (if you choose to believe it) part of the spear that pierced Jesus's side during the crucifixion. Many miraculous cures were claimed by the church. These relics disappeared during Henry VIII's suppression of the monasteries.

KIDMORE END ROAD,
EMMER GREEN

AT THE TURN of the last century Emmer Green was a self-contained village outside Caversham. This was the centre of that small community *c.* 1940. The shop was a relative newcomer; a

blacksmith had previously stood on that site since the sixteenth century. Until the 1920s the locals bought their groceries at the White Horse pub.

THE PUB AND the houses opposite survive to this day but the shop was redeveloped, set back to make room for the car-borne customer. Today, Emmer Green is very much a suburb of Reading rather than a free-standing village.

PROSPECT STREET,
CAVERSHAM

THIS DESERTED JUNCTION at the top of Prospect Street, Caversham, in about 1880 was more or less the end of the built-up area. The area was then known as Little End. The cottages on the left were destroyed by fire in 1907, and the blaze drew a huge crowd from miles around. Is that what they meant by people making their own entertainment in those days? In the distance, the buildings of Queen Anne's School can be seen through the trees.

TODAY, THE PRINCE of Wales pub car park sits on the site where the cottages once stood and traffic lights are essential to avoid rush-hour chaos. The built-up areas of Caversham now extend for over a mile in each direction and the traffic from them tends to focus on this junction.

BRIDGE STREET, CAVERSHAM

IN THE OLD photograph on the right, a
stagecoach or horse bus can be seen in
the distance and the street is decorated in
celebration of Queen Victoria's Golden Jubilee
in 1877. The people of Caversham celebrated
the Jubilee with a grand dinner at Balmore
House, which children and old folk attended
free of charge. There were entertainments,
sports (including such exotic events as the
bucket race and the menagerie race in which
a cat beat a duck at something or other!) and
commemorative medals for the children. The day
ended with torchlight parades and fireworks.

MIRACULOUSLY, THE MODERN view of Prospect Street (left) manages to capture one of those rare moments in the day when it is not gridlocked with traffic.

WESTFIELD ROAD RECREATION GROUND, CAVERSHAM

CAVERSHAM SCHOOLCHILDREN TURNED out in force to witness the opening of the Westfield Road playground in October 1930. The mayor, Councillor E.J. Venner, was personally behind the scheme, which he had promoted as a work creation programme for the town's unemployed. The mayor duly declared the area 'a children's paradise' and delighted his young audience by having a go on the rocking horse.

THE RECREATION GROUND continues to be a valued open space in the heart of Caversham with its cheerful flowerbeds and well kept green lawn. However, much of the 1930s play equipment would probably fall foul of modern health and safety standards.

CAVERSHAM LIBRARY

CAVERSHAM LIBRARY WAS one of many donated to communities around Britain and the USA by the Scottish-born self-made millionaire Andrew Carnegie. It was opened in 1907 and the photograph below is thought to have been taken on the opening day.

THE CHURCH NEXT to the Caversham library in the modern photograph used to be the Glendale cinema (and before that the Caversham Electric Theatre). The library itself stands on land which was once the playground to Caversham House Academy. The school itself was on the opposite side of Church Street where the shopping precinct now stands, and the two were linked by a tunnel under the road.

NEW LANE HILL,
TILEHURST

A FAVOURITE ACTIVITY for Edwardian children seems to have been standing about in the middle of the road to oblige photographers. This particular example was recorded in 1911 in Church Road (now New Lane Hill) Tilehurst.

TODAY, WALKING IN the middle of the road is called jay-walking and is punishable by being run over by a bus. St Michael's church, which can be seen in the background, dates back to the twelfth century. The oldest surviving part (the south aisle) is *c.* 1300. The church was much restored in 1855 and again a century later, and is notable for the spectacular early seventeenth-century tomb of one-time Lord of the Manor Sir Peter Vanlore and his family.

89

PROSPECT PARK POND

WITH NO LEISURE pools for children at the start of the twentieth century, this pond at Prospect Park may have been the best opportunity some of them ever had to play – or at to play least safely – in water. The old photograph on the left was taken soon after the park was acquired for the people of Reading by the council in 1901.

TODAY THERE ARE safer and cleaner places for children to swim, and the pond is gradually being reclaimed by nature.

CAVERSHAM ROAD

THE FLOODS OF 1894 inundated many parts of lower Caversham and reached as far south as the railway station. They were even worse than those of 1947. The picture below shows Caversham Road temporarily converted into the Venice of Berkshire.

OVER A CENTURY later and the street scene is little changed. Caversham Road had for centuries been particularly prone to regular flooding (hence its early name Watery Lane) until its level was raised in the 1720s. At its worst, Caversham was entirely cut off from Reading.

GREYFRIARS' CHURCH

GREYFRIARS' CHURCH HAS had a chequered history. Completed in 1311, it is said to be one of the most complete pieces of Franciscan architecture to survive in Britain. However, it was allowed to decay for centuries after its closure by Henry VIII in 1538. It served variously as the town's guildhall, hospital and finally a squalid and roofless prison before its restoration in 1863.

IN THE OLD photograph on the left the pre-restoration ruins can be seen. Prior to its restoration, Reading's Catholic community tried to buy it as their first place of worship in the town. But doctrinal differences prevented the sale taking place, and the Catholics ended up in the Pugin-designed St James' church next to the abbey ruins and the prison. As the new photograph shows, the church remains in ecclesiastical use today, though the names of some of the prisoners scratched into the pillars can still be seen, reminding us of its days as a prison.

Other titles published by The History Press

Haunted Berkshire
ROGER LONG

For such a small county, reports of supernatural happenings around Berkshire are surprisingly plentiful and varied. The haunting figures range from shades of kings, queens and dukes to apparitions of sobbing maidens and moaning men. They haunt all manner of places such as castles, mansions, churchyards, cottages, follies and grottoes. This intriguing and very readable volume contains numerous reported sightings of ghosts across one of the oldest counties in England.

978 0 7524 5907 3

A Berkshire Christmas
DAVID GREEN

A fascinating illustrated anthology, *A Berkshire Christmas* includes seasonal extracts from *A Wind in the Willows* by Kenneth Grahame, whose inspiration came largely from the Thames-side villages of Cookham and Pangbourne; a Christmas letter from Jane Austen, who went to school in Reading; and thoughts on Christmas customs from the prolific nineteenth-century Berkshire writer Peter H. Ditchfield and much more, making it the perfect stocking filler for anyone interested in the county.

978 0 7524 5333 0

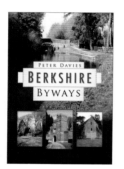

Berkshire Byways
PETER DAVIES

'If I were to list my principal hobbies', says author Peter Davies, 'they would include gawping: not idly or uselessly, but with awe.' Berkshire certainly has plenty to be awestruck about. Part history, part guide, this new book takes us on an appealing journey around the often overlooked county of Berkshire, offering many insights and surprises. However well you know the county, you will discover something new in these pages.

978 0 7509 4960 6

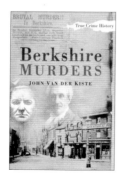

Berkshire Murders
JOHN VAN DER KISTE

Berkshire Murders is an examination of some of the country's most notorious and shocking cases. They include Hannah Carey, beaten to death by her husband at Warfield in 1851; young Hannah Gould, whose throat was cut by her father in a frenzied attack at Windsor in 1861; Nell Woodridge, murdered by her husband in 1896 and later immortalised in Oscar Wilde's 'The Ballad of Reading Gaol'; and Minnie Freeman Lee, whose body was discovered in a trunk in 1948. John Van der Kitse's well-illustrated and enthralling text will appeal to all those interested in the darker side of Berkshire's history.

978 0 7524 1619 9

Visit our website and discover thousands of other History Press books.

www.thehistorypress.co.uk